STRATEGY, NATIONAL INTERESTS, AND MEANS TO AN END

Stephen D. Sklenka

October 2007

_____

_____

*****

The views expressed in this report are those of the author and do not necessarily reflect the official policy or position of the Department of the Army, the Department of Defense, or the U.S. Government. This report is cleared for public release; distribution is unlimited.

*****

Comments pertaining to this report are invited and should be forwarded to: Director, Strategic Studies Institute, U.S. Army War College, 122 Forbes Ave, Carlisle, PA 17013-5244.

*****

All Strategic Studies Institute (SSI) publications are available on the SSI homepage for electronic dissemination. Hard copies of this report also may be ordered from our homepage. SSI's homepage address is: *www.StrategicStudiesInstitute.army.mil.*

*****

PREFACE

The U.S. Army War College provides an excellent environment for selected military officers and government civilians to reflect and use their career experience to explore a wide range of strategic issues. To assure that the research developed by Army War College students is available to Army and Department of Defense leaders, the Strategic Studies Institute publishes selected papers in its "Carlisle Papers in Security Strategy" Series.

ANTULIO J. ECHEVARRIA II
Director of Research
Strategic Studies Institute

ABOUT THE AUTHOR

STEPHEN D. SKLENKA, a Lieutenant Colonel in the U.S. Marine Corps, is the Commandant of the Marine Corps Fellow at the Center for Strategic and International Studies (CSIS). He is a logistics officer and a Marine Air-Ground Task Force planner. Lieutenant Colonel Sklenka was deployed in Operation JUST CAUSE in Panama, Marine Detachment UNITAS in South America, Operations DESERT SHIELD/DESERT STORM in Kuwait and Saudi Arabia, Operation RESTORE HOPE in Somalia, various exercises throughout southwest Asia and South Korea, Operation IRAQI FREEDOM, and Joint Task Force (JTF)-Katrina on the U.S Gulf Coast. He has commanded three companies, served as a regimental logistics officer, and worked at Headquarters Marine Corps in the Plans, Policies, and Operations Branch. Most recently, Lieutenant Colonel Sklenka commanded Marine Service Support Group (MSSG)-11 where he deployed with the 11th Marine Expeditionary Unit (Special Operations Capable) to the U.S. Gulf Coast in support of JTF-Katrina and with the 11th MEU (SOC) to the Pacific and Central Combatant Command regions. His next assignment is with the J-4 Plans of U.S. Special Operations Command. Lieutenant Colonel Sklenka graduated from the Amphibious Warfare School, Quantico, VA; and has a B.S. in history from the U.S. Naval Academy, Annapolis, MD; an M.A. in national security and strategic studies from the Naval Command and Staff College at the Naval War College, Newport, RI; and completed the Air War College Non-Resident Program.

ABSTRACT

This paper focuses on the interrelationship among national interests, stated ends, means to achieve those ends, and the strategies required to tie all of them together into a cohesive and effective vision for the commitment of U.S. forces. The introduction addresses the current U.S. debate regarding proposed actions in the Iraq War and postulates that the lack of true strategic discussion, particularly by our national leadership who instead prefer to focus on far less appropriate discussions such as tactics and techniques, inhibits the development of a comprehensive and effective overarching vision and ultimately is to blame for the setbacks that the U.S.-led coalition has experienced in Iraq. This lack of strategic foresight, however, is not surprising and has become endemic to American foreign policy since the end of the Cold War. The fact that so much of U.S. post-Cold War foreign policy involves interventions merely exacerbates the difficulties a lack of strategic foresight engenders. The U.S. inability☐ or unwillingness☐ to connect strategic ends and appropriate means to accomplish clearly defined goals has occurred so often over the past 15 years that one could make a credible argument that it has become a disturbing and pervasive characteristic of the modern American way of war.

The first section briefly explains the theoretical concepts behind the development of ends, means, and strategy. Understanding the manner in which ends, means, and strategy relate to one another is crucial toward developing a national vision, particularly when determining whether an intervention of U.S. military forces may or may not be mandated.

Once the basic theoretical construct is explained, that design is placed against four recent interventional actions in which the United States has participated: Somalia, the Balkans, Haiti, and Iraq. In each of these cases, an examination of the declared stated ends is conducted, an assessment of the means dedicated to achieving those ends is made, and a look at the overall strategy tying those ends and means together is performed.

The paper concludes by asserting that the strategic failures that occurred within the four recent interventions are not coincidental. Rather, they represent predictable outcomes that are to be expected when strategic vision is lacking. Clear, succinct, and obtainable ends must be articulated by national leadership prior to the commitment of force to ensure that force is actually representative of appropriate and corresponding means to achieve those ends. Moreover, only a unified strategic design can ensure that the means are properly employed and that the ends remain focused☐ especially when the environment changes in such a way as to engender a necessary adjustment to those ends that require a commensurate adjustment in dedicated means as well.

Accordingly, the principal lesson to be learned is that when the United States commits its military forces in support of interventions, success can only be achieved if clear ends are identified, appropriate means are leveraged against those stated ends, and a coherent strategy is developed to coordinate the ends and means. While such a statement can be dismissed as common sense, our recent history clearly demonstrates that such is certainly not the case.

STRATEGY, NATIONAL INTERESTS, AND MEANS TO AN END

> No one starts a war — or rather, no one in his senses ought to do so — without first being clear in his mind what he intends to achieve by that war and how he intends to conduct it.

> Carl von Clausewitz[1]

Introduction.

> To know in war how to recognize an opportunity and seize it is better than anything else.

> Niccolo Machiavelli, *The Art of War*[2]

The United States is currently in the midst of a pivotal struggle. Numerous terms have been proffered to describe this conflict; The Global War on Terrorism (GWOT), the Long War, the Struggle against Islamic Extremism, and the Fight against Global Jihadism are among the most popular appellations. Within this struggle, the conflict taking place in Iraq has undeniably assumed center stage. Whether one believes Iraq to be the central front in this global battle or one believes that the present situation arose out of U.S. actions that have created a self-fulfilling prophecy is immaterial. The point is that the United States is heavily engaged in that nation and will undoubtedly remain active there for some time to come. Accordingly, success is predicated upon the development of a sound, comprehensive, and resourced strategy. However, the development of that strategy has proven to be immensely challenging. Given America's recent history with interventions, this quandary is not surprising; our nation routinely has had difficulty connecting desired ends to the necessary means required to achieve those ends with the result being the execution of uncoordinated and unfocused strategies.

There is an old adage that is especially apt when discussing the multitude of strategic options regarding Iraq: If you do not know where you are going, then any road will get you there. The truth in that adage becomes more apparent as numerous proposals regarding "the best" course of action for the United States to take in Iraq continue to be advocated and deliberated. The past few months in particular have witnessed a vociferous debate regarding the subject of strategic direction. Choruses of "Stay the Course" and "Cut and Run" monopolized virtually every foreign policy discussion prior to the November 2006 congressional elections. Some have argued since the first day of the war that insufficient numbers of forces have been employed in Iraq; increasing troop strength is seen by many who hold this view as a requirement if a favorable solution is to be achieved. Many counter that position by claiming that there simply are not sufficient forces available within the U.S. inventory to add for an extended period in Iraq. Meanwhile, others passionately espouse the belief that the only viable course of action remaining for the United States is a withdrawal of our forces from the battle zone. Proponents of this plan are convinced that our forces are caught in the middle of a situation that has deteriorated beyond the ability of our military to fix. Then there are the "middle" options. The most oft-cited alternatives within this category include a call for the strategic redeployment of forces to areas outside Iraq but within regional proximity, as well as a plan to forge a federated partition of Iraq—the so-called "Biden-Gelb Plan" or variations thereof.

However, lost amid the din of these highly charged debates and arguments is perhaps the most fundamental element of strategy itself. The one question that requires an answer in order to make the strategic debate relevant essentially has not been asked: *What is the U.S. desired end state in Iraq?* In other words, what are the U.S. political goals for Iraq? In an attempt to answer this question last year, the White House published the *National Strategy for Victory in Iraq (NSVI)*, and since publication, no other official documents have countermanded the goals stated in that document. Specifically, the *NSVI* identified three principal objectives:

- Short Term: Iraq is making steady progress in fighting terrorists, meeting political milestones, building democratic institutions, and standing up security forces.
- Medium Term: Iraq is in the lead defeating terrorists and providing its own security with a fully constitutional government in place and is on its way to achieving its economic potential.
- Longer Term: Iraq is peaceful, united, stable, and secure, well integrated into the international community, and a full partner in the global war on terrorism.[3]

More than a year later, the fundamental question that requires answering is whether or not these ends are still valid. Is it still in the U.S. best interests to commit manpower, treasure, and resources toward the attainment of these specific objectives? Unfortunately, such questions have been overlooked or at least obscured as the nation plods along in search of a strategy that will enable American forces to ultimately be extricated from Iraq.

While a national debate regarding strategic direction is certainly required—and long overdue—such a debate cannot really exist without first conducting serious discussions regarding the desired end state vis-à-vis Iraq. All talk of strategic options prior to the determination of political goals is not only premature; it is counterproductive. Any meaningful debate of strategy is essentially amorphous since there is nothing of substance on which it can adequately focus. Current discussions regarding proposed strategic directions are only appropriate if the political aims as identified in the White House's *NSVI* remain unchanged. However, discussions regarding the continued viability of those objectives have been completely overshadowed by discourse that has focused almost exclusively on strategy.

Focusing the discussion principally on strategy metaphorically puts the cart before the horse. Strategy without an aiming point represented by a defined end state is doomed to drift aimlessly. Establishing a clearly defined set of political goals up front, though, enables the formulation of an executable strategy and the identification of requisite means designed to support that strategy. Success hinges on that critical first step—determination of the end state. Only after that determination is accomplished can a meaningful strategy and the allocation of appropriate resources to achieve that strategy occur. The process conceptually is rather simple—ends must first be determined, a strategy is then developed, and finally, appropriate means to conduct that strategy to achieve the desired ends are identified and allocated. Iraq is proving, however, that theory and execution often are not cooperative partners, as the stated ends have not necessarily corresponded to the actual means committed. That ends-means mismatch has in turn posed predictable challenges to the development of a coherent strategy vis-à-vis Iraq. This situation should not be a surprise, though, because recent U.S. history provides several examples where ends-means mismatches have become alarmingly pervasive. The U.S. inability☐ or unwillingness☐ to connect strategic ends and appropriate means to accomplish those ends has occurred so often over the past 15 years that one could make a credible argument that it has become a disturbing and pervasive characteristic of the modern American way of war. Examining specific cases from the previous decade as well as Operation IRAQI FREEDOM validates this point, but first, a review of the relationship among ends, means, and overall strategy is in order.

Ends, Means, and the Design of Strategy.

> Strategy depends for success, first and most, on a sound calculation and coordination of the end and the means.

B. H. Liddell Hart[4]

Military theorists over the years have offered numerous definitions for the terms strategy, ends, and means. While the numbers of definitions are in as much abundance as the philosophers who furnish them, a commonality within the basic premise of the words tends to dominate, particularly in the contemporary era. The key is tying the terms together in a manner that demonstrates the mutually supportive role each possesses relative to the others. One such definition neatly conveys the symmetry that conceptually exists among strategy, ends, and means. For the purposes of this paper, strategy is defined as a "complex decisionmaking process that connects the ends sought (objectives) with the ways and means of achieving those ends."[5] Strategy relates means to ends and encompasses the process by which the means, expressed as instruments of national power, are employed to accomplish stated ends that are expressed as the national interests. In other words, strategy represents the intellectual connection among "the things one wants to achieve, the means at hand, and the circumstances."[6]

Strategy requires the assemblage and coordination of specified acts deliberately linked together in a manner designed to achieve a specific end or set of ends. Under this specification, concepts such as anticommunism, maritime superiority, the cultivation of alliances, and information dominance represent desires and goals, not, as they are often erroneously termed, strategies.[7] Tangible objectives are the target of legitimate strategies, posing a fundamental difference from ideas and dreams. The objectives, or ends, of strategy are represented by national interests, and it is here where much consternation and debate among political leadership occurs. Defining national interests is a challenge in and of itself. Such definition "demands the willingness of a state to uphold its morals and national values with the commitment of its blood, treasure, time, and energy to achieve sometimes specific and sometimes inspecific ends."[8]

Accordingly, the multiple variances in ideology within this country interact to create an often contentious process when attempting to identify ends worthy of national commitment. Although national interests provide a broad construct within which political leaders can guide their decisions, they are also representative of the citizenry's ideals.[9] The diversity of the United States, a trait contributing to its enduring strength, understandably makes achieving consensus regarding overarching national ideals difficult at best. Moreover, failure to identify the parameters of the discussion or state the "rules of the game" up front invariably leads to incorrectly prioritizing interests, i.e., ends, that cause incomplete strategies to be developed using inappropriate means. Accordingly, common terminology that is agreed upon throughout the policymaking community is essential to ensure that strategic development is properly focused.

Political scientist Donald Neuchterlein developed a template that offers four versions of national interest that are based on relative intensity. Figure 1 provides a graphical representation of that framework.

	Intensity of Interest			
	Survival	Vital	Major	Peripheral
Defense of Homeland				
Economic Well-being				
Favorable World Order				
Promotion of Values				

(Basic Interest at Stake)

(Adapted from Donald Neuchterlein, "National Interests and National Strategy," in Terry L. Heyns, ed., *Understanding U.S. Strategy: A Reader*, Washington, DC: National Defense University, 1983, p. 38.

Figure 1. National Interest Matrix.[10]

Specific interests are prioritized from highest to lowest along the vertical axis under the header, "Basic Interest at Stake," and the significance of that interest is listed under the header "Intensity of Interest" along the horizontal axis. As previously stated, defining the criteria that establishes a particular intensity of interest is certainly a challenge, and the manner in which national leadership defines those terms is perhaps the single most important element in the overall development of national strategy. Such definition enables consistency to be applied in determining what actions and means are necessary to achieve which desired ends. The definition of a "survival" interest is pretty clear cut; a nation's physical existence is threatened by an attack. The use of military force is unquestionably advanced in support of survival interests. Next on the intensity scale are "vital" interests where serious harm to the nation occurs unless dealt with using strong measures, including force. Nations are unwilling to compromise these interests; the maintenance of territorial integrity is an example of a vital national interest. "Major" interests are next on the intensity scale. Similar to vital interests, a primary difference between the two is that use of force is not deemed necessary in the defense of major interests. Nations tend not to go to war over major interests; they will do so over vital interests, though. Finally, "peripheral" interests impact a nation's overall interests but do not really pose a threat to the nation as a whole.

Debate regarding the use of military force is not generally required when addressing survival and peripheral interests. The requirement or lack thereof is usually self-evident. However, the line differentiating vital from major interests is blurred more often than not, and it is in this region that identifying appropriate strategy, ends, and means proves to be the most challenging. Assessing a nation☐s or region☐s importance to the United States is a crucial step in determining what level of interest a particular issue represents. Equally critical is determining if a concomitant commitment of U.S. forces is required to protect those interests. In all but survival interests, ends are governed greatly by the means available to accomplish them. This reality heightens the contention among those advocating that a particular interest be designated as either vital or major, since limited resources required in dedication of the pursuit of particular national objectives must be redirected from support to other issues (e.g., domestic social programs). Ultimately, the public☐s willingness to commit force often depends on its interpretation of a given threat. Just as often, the effectiveness of the political leadership to convince their constituents one way or the other regarding the use of force can be the determining factor in moving a particular interest from a major to a vital interest or vice versa. Complicating matters, general agreement regarding the designation of a particular interest as "vital" does not necessarily result in a consensus regarding how to protect that interest.[11] Constant vigilance in the application of these definitions when determining strategy is essential if an ends-means match is to occur, and an attendant strategy to tie those ends and means together is to be developed. If national political leadership confuses these definitions, a confused strategy with conflicting ends will inevitably result.

The U.S. Government Accountability Office (GAO) has conducted research and published numerous reports in the past that have identified the six most desirable characteristics of a national strategy. The points listed in Figure 2 offer policymakers a beneficial tool in ensuring accountability and in achieving effective results when crafting strategy.[12]

---

1. A clear purpose, scope, methodology.
2. A detailed discussion of the problems, risks, and threats the strategy intends to address.
3. The desired goals and objectives, and outcome-related performance measures.
4. A description of the U.S. resources needed to implement the strategy.
5. A clear delineation of the U.S. government roles, responsibilities, and mechanisms for coordination.
6. A description of how the strategy is integrated internally among U.S. agencies and externally with allies.

Figure 2. Six Characteristics of a Desirable National Strategy.

As indicated in Figure 2, a coherent strategy begins with the identification of a desired objective or end. Understanding purposes and objectives will not guarantee victory, but failure to understand them virtually guarantees defeat.[13] Essentially, answering the question, "What do I really want out of this situation?"[14] puts national leadership on the path toward establishing meaningful ends. When determining if military intervention is necessary, defining an end is a nation's method of declaring that a particular objective is worth sacrificing its blood and treasure to achieve. Angelo Codevilla and Paul Seabury offer a series of subsequent questions that assist policymakers in refining their ends, identifying requisite means to achieve those ends, and developing a suitable strategy that ties the ends and means together. The questions provided in Figure 3 indicate that the process of ends-means matching and strategic development are not one-time events but rather require continual reassessment to ensure that the necessary symmetry among the three is maintained. [15]

---

1. Whom or what do I have to kill, destroy, besiege, intimidate, or constrain to get what I want?" Once these things are accomplished, will I have achieved my desired ends? Will this obtain "victory?"
2. What can my enemy do to keep from accomplishing those actions of killing, destroying, etc.?
3. What forces do I have to achieve my desired ends? Can I expand my forces and contract my enemy's?
4. Do I possess the requisite will to achieve my desired ends? Have I realistically calculated the anticipated costs associated with executing this war, and if so, am I willing to commit those resources toward my stated ends?
5. What kind of peace do I want to achieve?
6. What actions must I accomplish in order to remove any obstacles in the path toward the type of peace I desire?
7. What must I do to avoid defeat?
8. What must I do to defeat the enemy's will?

Figure 3. Ends-Means Matching and Strategic Development.

Consideration of these questions throughout an intervention enables policymakers to ensure that they are correctly focused on their own actions as well as those of the enemy. Each can be linked to the overall stated ends, and equally as important, each also can be traced back to the issue of means and strategy necessary to accomplish those ends.

As an intervention proceeds and progresses, these questions also assist policymakers in framing the evaluations that are necessary to ensure the continued relevance of the initially stated ends. An important point to remember is that ends identified at the conception of an intervention are not necessarily cast in stone; policymakers are obligated to conduct periodic critiques regarding the continuing legitimacy and viability of ends regarding overall national policy. Clausewitz's declaration that the supremacy of the political aim over all others does not necessarily mean that upon initiation of hostilities political objectives cannot be altered. Military actions on the ground may actually create situations where adjustments to overarching political objectives must be considered.[16] Supremacy of the political objective should in no way translate into political obstinacy.

Adjusting ends, however, can be taken to extremes that prove counterproductive in their own right. While shrewd political leaders recognize instances where certain developments within an intervention may necessitate adjustments to objectives, they are wise to avoid chasing battlefield victories. Such action potentially results in unwarranted shifts of overarching political objectives.[17] The situation is exacerbated when those shifts are initially indiscernible, but as they compound, result in a seemingly sudden and drastic shift in political objectives that actually evolved over the course of incremental installments.

American policymakers have long wrestled with the numerous and disparate dynamics associated with forging a strategy to accomplish desired ends within the parameters of sound means allocation. The veracity of this reality has been illuminated even more clearly in the post-Cold War world. When the Soviet Union disbanded in 1991, the U.S. victory was paradoxically tainted. No longer does the United States possess the "luxury" of a well-defined opponent. Whereas questions regarding the efficacy of interventional actions once were relatively easily answered, especially when directed in response to Soviet actions, that level of clarity has since been markedly obscured. An examination of a few of the interventions in which this nation has participated either unilaterally or as leader of a multinational force over the past 15 years illustrates both the desideratum of an integrated and sound end-means match with accompanying strategy as well as the deleterious consequences that result when an imbalance among ends, means, and strategy occurs.

Somalia on the Periphery.

Do not act unwillingly nor selfishly nor without self-examination, nor with divergent motives.

Marcus Aurelius[18]

Somalia's descent into chaos is well-chronicled in several publications, so additional diagnosis of the nature of that tragedy is not required here. Analysis of how the United States got involved in that country, though, is germane to the issue of matching suitable ends to appropriate means and developing sound strategic design. The U.S. intervention into Somalia officially began with the declaration of the United Nations (UN) Security Council in the form of Resolution (UNSCR) 794 on December 3, 1992.[19] While not specifically citing the United States by name, "the offer of a member state" to lead a multinational task force was referenced in the resolution. The George H. W. Bush administration articulated relatively clear and well-defined ends in support of this Unified Task Force (UNITAF) operating under the rubric of Operation RESTORE HOPE. The purpose of America's foray was limited to the protection of food convoys and the disarming of clans in order to establish an environment conducive for the rapid turnover of humanitarian issues to a UN-led force identified as United Nations Operation in Somalia (UNOSOM).[20] American involvement was strictly limited to humanitarian actions and was to specifically avoid political interplay. Supply routes for the transport of food were to be opened, and conditions set for a rapid turnover to UN forces. A force of approximately 25,000 Americans, supplemented by an additional contingent of approximately 12,000 multinationals, was allocated in support of those limited ends.[21] Strict adherence to a code of neutrality was advertised, and U.S. forces made it clear that they had no intention of making war with any particular Somali clan.

The U.S.-led UNITAF appeared ostensibly to represent a text-book humanitarian mission, one whose employment certainly did not meet the established ideas of a survival or vital interest. Moreover, one could make a compelling case that Somalia did not represent a major national interest, either, and that as a peripheral national interest, the intervention of military forces violated the basic criteria established for governing such action. The Bush administration, however, curtailed dissent by justifying the mission on the grounds of humanitarian concerns. With mass media feeding the American public a steady diet of starvation and misery from the Horn of Africa region, President Bush did not have difficulty making his case to the American people.

While few could argue the merits of the first half of UNSCR 794's declared ends, the second half should have sent up significant warning signs to U.S. policymakers. Paragraph 10 of the resolution included a provision authorizing the use of "all necessary means to establish as soon as possible a secure environment for humanitarian relief operations in Somalia."[22] The obvious implication that force would be necessary in the execution of humanitarian actions was inconsistent with U.S. initially stated ends. Standard peacekeeping arrangements were already being violated by entering Somalia without invitation of the formal government, but that technicality was overlooked due to the absence of any central authority in that county. The intervention nonetheless still heightened tensions between the interventional force and the various clans; advocating the use of force in the execution of duties served to exacerbate an already agitated situation. While Bush addressed the humanitarian intentions of the mission, the UN not so subtly conveyed a more aggressive posture. The U.S. was never fully committed to the idea of weapons confiscation that the UN advocated because the scale of that involvement required far greater resources than the administration was willing to commit, and this disagreement with the UN indicated a developing ends-means mismatch within the operation that required the attention of national leadership to correct.

The altruistic nature of the intervention was corrupted by the requirement for U.S.-led forces to disarm the populace in concert with their mission to stem the starvation; like it or not, that provision implied a requirement to take sides and conduct combat operations. While the means applied against the humanitarian support side of the mission matched the stated ends, the mismatch occurred when balanced against the additional requirement to disarm an entire country possessed of a plethora of heavy weaponry. The means necessary to accomplish the particular stated end of disarmament could have required the intervening forces to engage and kill thousands of militiamen who were interspersed among the Somali population.[23] Obviously, those means would have contradicted the very notion of a humanitarian operation, and quite understandably, none of the nations involved in the intervention were willing to commit to an act that would have undoubtedly resulted in a tremendous amount of bloodshed. However, the stated end of disarmament was never rescinded. While the effects of this ends-means mismatch would not rear its ugly head during the execution of UNITAF, once the UN assumed command with UNOSOM II, the fateful effects were put on full display.

With the passing of command from UNITAF to UNOSOM II, there appeared to be a sense within the United States that the responsibility for continual analysis of the ends, means, and overall strategy was reduced. However, American forces, while reduced in quantity and not in charge of overall operations, remained in Somalia. Accordingly, it was incumbent on the new Clinton administration to ensure that a harmonious relationship existed among the ends, means, and overall strategy of the UN operations, at least as far as U.S. participation was involved. The first clue that an ends-means mismatch was inevitable should have been apparent when UNSCR 814, the resolution that authorized UNOSOM II, was published.

The UN decided that its force for UNOSOM II required enforcement powers authorized under Chapter VII[24] of the UN Charter in order to deal effectively with the warring clans, and UNSCR 814 possessed requisite provisions that radically altered the fundamental purpose of the humanitarian mission.[25] The two principal objectives of UNSCR 814 were for the UN to provide for the "consolidation, expansion, and maintenance of a secure environment throughout Somalia" and for "the rehabilitation of the political institutions and economy of Somalia."[26] Both of those ends stood in marked contrast to the stated ends that U.S. political leadership had identified at the beginning of the intervention. While ends and objectives are certainly malleable and should be adjusted as circumstances require, such alterations require a commensurate adaptation of the dedicated means assigned to accomplish the newly adjusted ends. In the case of UNOSOM II, however, that adjustment in means did not accompany the shift in ends. The case for an increase in means that reflected the altered ends could not have been more clear, either. With the inclusion of Chapter VII powers in UNOSOM II's charter, the humanitarian force was placed in a virtual state of war with the Somali clans, and U.S. forces were caught in the middle as their initial intent to avoid involvement with clan warfare issues was superseded by the passage of UNSCR 814.

The issue was further exacerbated when Mohammed Farah Aideed and his clan were explicitly identified as a target of U.S. and UN forces. The United States had firmly and blatantly taken sides in an intercommunal struggle about which they possessed minimal detailed knowledge. Additionally, with the identification of a specific "enemy," the declared ends of the operation shifted yet again, albeit unofficially. However, as with the previous adjustment in ends for the Somalia enterprise, no commensurate shift in means occurred. More disturbingly, though, there was no detailed analysis of how attacking Aideed fit into the overall strategic picture.[27] Once eliminated, his Habr Gidr clan undoubtedly would have found a new leader, and even if his clan was defeated, another would certainly have taken its place. No strategic explanation was ever provided that indicated why Aideed was specifically targeted.

Moreover, not only did the new Clinton administration not seem to be overly concerned with the sharp deviation in ends and appeared equally unmindful of the new environment in which the UN had definitively placed American forces, they celebrated the undeniable escalation of the mission. Commenting in a joint U.S.-UN press release shortly after the pronouncement of UNSCR 814, the U.S. Ambassador to the UN proclaimed that the new resolution represented □an unprecedented enterprise aimed at nothing less than the restoration of an entire country."[28] With the stroke of a pen, the United States had enthusiastically been convinced to follow the UN into making the significant leap from humanitarian assistance to full scale nation-building. A mission that initially was identified as a simple humanitarian operation morphed into an action that called for essentially a "transformation of society."[29] However, no attendant increase in force commitment or resource allocation followed the new, lofty ends. The U.S. national leadership believed that the introduction of additional forces would result in an escalation of hostilities within Somalia, and they did not desire a war, particularly over a peripheral or major national interest. Unfortunately, the stated ends for the mission that they accepted demanded essentially just that. Predictably, the failure to synchronize appropriate means to the amorphous and shifting ends of the operation resulted in unavoidable difficulties in the execution of the overall mission, and U.S. forces were among those who paid in blood for the oversight.

The ends in Somalia continued to evolve, with the Clinton administration expanding the basic set of objectives initially articulated as a result of the evolving situation on the ground. Such revision is certainly commendatory, but unless accompanied by a full analysis of associated requirements to meet the expanded ends, the action can prove fatal to an operation. In late August 1993, Secretary of Defense Les Aspin gave a speech at the Center for Strategic and International Studies in Washington, DC, where he identified additional actions that required accomplishment prior to the withdrawal of U.S. forces from Somalia. These new requirements included the restoration of order in Mogadishu, progress in the efforts to disarm the warlords, and establishing legitimate police forces in the major population centers.[30] By the time of Aspin's speech, the United States had fundamentally altered its stated desired ends regarding Somalia. While observers cite this shift as the most significant contribution to what is commonly referred to as a "failed" mission, such an assertion is only half correct. Had the shift in ends been accompanied by an attendant adjustment in means to accomplish those ends, many of the challenges that U.S. forces faced in Somalia during the autumn of 1993 would have been avoided. As the ends changed, strategic planners at the national leadership level were obligated to conduct an analysis of the evolving situation to determine what shifts in means were necessary to accommodate the requirements of the newly stated ends and then act on their findings. The lack of any substantive action designed to match means with new ends predictably resulted in ultimate failure of the mission.

Many argue that the political climate in 1993 did not lend itself to a commitment of additional forces in support of a UN-led humanitarian and nation-building action. Accordingly, no additional authorities of Congress were requested in order to meet the needs of this mission shift.[31] That may certainly have been true, and Clausewitz does remind his readers that, "We can only treat policy as representative of all interests of the community."[32] However, if the policy could not accept an increase in means, then the policy leaders were obligated to scale back their desired ends to more accurately reflect the reality of the means dedicated toward their achievement.

After 18 U.S. soldiers were killed during a battle in Mogadishu in early October 1993, a reversal of ends was announced. President Clinton declared in an October 7 speech entitled *Address to the Nation on Somalia* that "It is not our job to rebuild Somalia's society," completely reversing his previous policy that embraced nation-building in that country.[33] While ultimately increasing troop numbers by about 5,000 for a 6-month period, this augmentation of means was again balanced against mismatched ends since that force essentially served as an internally focused force protection entity, contributing little to the actual adjusted ends of temporarily resuming simple humanitarian support for a 6-month period.

Throughout the Somalia mission, particularly once the Clinton administration took office, an ends-means mismatch consistently resulted in ends and means chasing shifting policies. As policymakers continually refined the ends, they neglected to conduct the necessary analysis to refine and commit the means to achieve those ends. The consequence of an ends-means mismatch and the attendant disjointed strategy combined to create a situation where manpower and resources were sacrificed in the pursuit of ill-defined policy objectives. Ultimately, this contributed to the operation being deemed a "failure" simply because of the manner in which the United States withdrew from Somalia. The "failure" was not in the operation itself, as thousands of Somalis were saved due to U.S. and UN interventional actions. Rather, the failure was more accurately due to the national leadership's inability to develop sound strategy that appreciated the necessity of an ends-means match.

Strategic Pitfalls of a Balkanizing Policy.

If 20 soldiers were killed tomorrow in a terrorist bombing in Bosnia, the Clinton administration would have to invent, generally from scratch, a national interest for being there.

Robert D. Kaplan
Balkan Ghosts: A Journey Through History[34]

The 1990s were not kind to the Balkan region. Yugoslavia did not dissolve at the end of the Cold War; it imploded. Long simmering ethnic differences exploded in a caldron of rage that approached genocide. Unable to agree on any coordinated or unified action, the international community settled on a policy of inaction, at least for the first couple of years, and the conflict in Bosnia threatened to rage out of control with a very real potential for metastasizing throughout southern Europe. Within the United States specifically, a lack of national consensus prevented the Bush administration from taking decisive interventional steps during the initial days of calamity in Bosnia. Desired ends could not be agreed upon, and so a policy devoid of any meaningful involvement of U.S. forces was advocated. When the Clinton administration took office in early 1993, its rhetoric regarding the exigency was more forceful than that of its predecessors, but its initial actions were not.[35]

During a stump speech as the Democratic Party's presidential candidate, William Jefferson Clinton gave the world a glimpse into the coming lack of strategic foresight that his administration would display regarding Bosnia. Believing that all human rights violations merit international investigation, then-candidate Clinton asserted that, "We may have to use force" in order to resolve instances of human rights abuses. Continuing, he stated that ☐ would begin with air power against the Serbs to try and restore the basic conditions of humanity."[36] This was clearly an indication of the inability to understand the basic requirement to match ends and means. The idea that air power would restore "basic conditions of humanity" indicates a lack of appreciation for the means necessary to achieve otherwise nobly stated ends.

Ultimately, U.S. leadership could not decide on exactly what the desired ends regarding Bosnia were. The key questions that demand answering when determining ends and developing strategy were never asked:
- What do I really want out of this situation?
- What will victory look like?
- What forces do I have to achieve my desired ends?
- Do I possess the requisite will to achieve my desired ends?
- What kind of peace do I want to achieve?

Failure to answer those questions resulted in a situation where the U.S. policy appeared to "flounder" endlessly. While the U.S. Ambassador to the UN led a chorus within

Congress in advocating unilateral air strikes against Serbia, the administration vacillated, threatening action but repeatedly pulling back from committing any acts of real substance.[37] While their faith in the diplomatic process is admirable, it was also prudent given their inability to agree on any firm ends for the conflict. An argument can certainly be made that their sensible posture was arrived at by fortuitous happenstance rather than through careful calculation of national interests, ends, and means; the dissonance among the administration's policymakers prevented action from occurring. Regardless, not rushing to action worked to the administration's benefit, as that stance bought them time to forge a more rational and balanced ends, means, and strategy design.

Because of the demonstrated lack of resolve by the intervening nations in escalating the conflict, the Serbian leadership decided that they could send additional forces into Bosnia without worrying about leaving Serbia relatively unprotected. The Serbs were convinced that the intervening forces were not going to move against them, and the Croats were not strong enough to mount a credible offensive against Serbia. In essence, the Serb leadership interpreted the stated desire of intervening nations led by the United States to resist direct involvement in hostilities with the Balkan factions as a lack of resolve. Ironically, a position of neutrality ostensibly taken to enhance cooperation among adversaries merely fueled hostilities by providing windows of vulnerability for the Serbs to exploit.[38]

After the notorious mortar attack on a Sarajevo marketplace, Congressional outcry demanded some meaningful action be taken regarding Bosnia. A policy of four components—avoiding a broader European war, preserving NATO's credibility, stemming the flow of refugees, and halting the slaughter of innocents in Bosnia—was mandated. The achievement of those ends obviously required a substantial commitment of national means, yet the Clinton administration was reluctant to commit the necessary resources. The ends-means mismatch contributed to the inevitability of an escalating conflict. Responding to the public demands for substantive action, the Clinton administration was compelled to reconsider its approach to the achievement of its stated ends. Accordingly, the United States, working through NATO, threatened attacks against Serbian leadership if Serbian forces persisted in perpetuating the humanitarian crisis.[39]

The case for intervention was certainly compelling, but doing so in response to public condemnation rather than out of adherence to a set policy invariably leads to the formation of an unfocused strategy developed without full analysis of the situation. A credible argument can be made that the intervening forces led by the United States inadvertently proved counterproductive in one key respect and actually prolonged the Balkan conflicts. That the intervening forces sought peace is undeniable, but what was never fully addressed was what type of peace was actually sought. The fundamental issue of ends was left unresolved as intervening nations could not determine whose cause to support or which peace to advocate. The only high-level aspect on which all agreed was a strict adherence to a code of neutrality. Declaring also that they would not be coerced into using force, the intervening forces presented the impression to some that their true ends were geared more toward ensuring their own safety than toward achieving any decisive results. The insistence on simply separating warring parties rather than attempting to impose some version of an enduring peace contributed to an incessant indecisiveness among the political leadership of the intervening forces whose continual inability to agree on tangible ends prevented the development of a unified strategy.

Even in attaining a cessation of hostilities, "victory" could hardly be claimed by the U.S.-led coalition. When the Dayton Accords ended the conflict by creating a Bosnian state, there were still three viable—and adversarial—armies within close proximity of each other. Not surprisingly, the failure to unite ends, means, and a strategic vision for the Balkans seems to have unwittingly perpetuated the conflict.[40] While the slaughter of innocents in Bosnia has been curtailed, concern persists that a complete withdrawal of the interventional force would be accompanied shortly thereafter by a resumption of the horrors that caused the intervention into Bosnia in the first place. Fifteen years later, the situation has not progressed adequately enough to convince the European Union (EU), custodians of the interventional forces in Bosnia since December of 2004, that disengagement would not be followed by disastrous consequences. Additionally, the lack of a unified strategic design enabled the dominant Serb army to remain a potent force in the region. The intervening forces' devotion to neutrality, coupled with their attendant refusal to reduce or destroy the Serb military, produced the unintended consequence of contributing to the successor regional conflict in Kosovo by preserving the means of the aggressor for that event.

A compelling case can be made that the failure to adequately address Serb forces in Bosnia merely delayed the inevitability that was realized a few years later in Kosovo. As with the ends in Bosnia, cessation of Serb aggression represented the primary aim of the United States. The means for achieving that end consisted primarily of U.S.-led North Atlantic Treaty Organization (NATO) air strikes against Serbia. While the means employed in Kosovo were deemed appropriate for that particular conflict, once again a lack of an overarching strategy that related the end and means to a broader U.S. vision for the world created unintended consequences. Russia and China were unsurprisingly quite irritated with U.S. actions vis-à-vis Kosovo, particularly since they were dealing with their own set of disgruntled minorities in the form of the Chechens and Tibetans respectively.[41] Interestingly, the ends identified regarding Kosovo did not necessarily fit the profile of "vital" national interest, yet U.S. ends and accompanying strategies impacting Russia and China routinely fell into that category.

Moreover, many within the rest of the international community viewed U.S. actions regarding Kosovo as both confusing and conflicting. Chechens and Tibetans were left to wonder why the United States seemed to neglect their plight yet embrace that of the Kosovars. One analyst took this inconsistency further in asserting that the United States demonstrated an apparent lack of genuine commitment regarding the rights of others with its reluctance to take casualties in Somalia, and that the image of U.S. moral credibility was severely strained due to the lack of substantive action to prevent the decade⬚s ⬚greatest atrocity" in Rwanda.[42] In the cases of Somalia, Rwanda, and even Tibet or Chechnya, national leadership determined that the desired ends regarding those regions simply were not worth applying the necessary means. As long as the national leadership does not designate human rights and associated humanitarian issues as vital or even major national interests, one cannot expect means normally associated with those types of interests to be applied. While such a policy may not be popular, in actuality, it does help ensure against the development of strategies with attendant ends-means mismatches. Unfortunately, inconsistent policies in the application of certain means, predominantly the use of military force, more often than not result from poor strategic vision and the absence of a careful regard for how varying policies interact with one another to create global effects.[43]

Haiti and the American Backyard.

With the movements in this hemisphere we are of necessity more immediately connected, and by causes which must be obvious to all enlightened and impartial observers.

President James Monroe
Seventh Annual Message to Congress
December 2, 1823[44]

Debate regarding Haiti's place within U.S. national interests has raged for well over a century. Based on American actions, however, the logical conclusion is that the United States does possess a national security interest in Haiti, but that the interest is not vital.[45] American policy has traditionally identified two principal interests regarding Haiti — the promotion of democracy, and the encouragement of conditions of stability so that Haitians would be more inclined to remain at home rather than immigrate in mass numbers to the United States.[46]

President Clinton's decision to intervene in Haiti in 1994 appears to have been driven more by domestic pressures than actual concern over the conditions in Haiti. While sympathies for the miserable humanitarian situation within that island nation certainly elicited some sympathies, the real threat to the United States came in the form of an increasing flow to American shores of Haitian refugees desperate to leave their island.[47] While a candidate for the presidency, Clinton decried the policies of then-President George H. W. Bush regarding Haiti. Specifically, he condemned the forced repatriation of Haitians who sought asylum in the United States, and he promised to repeal the repatriation policy if elected. Once in office, though, that promise was rescinded as the Clinton administration became concerned about intelligence reports that warned of over 200,000 Haitian refugees who were preparing to depart for U.S. shores.[48] Deciding that a virtual repetition of the 1980 Mariel boatlift would create enormous electoral damage, the new President decided that a continuation of his predecessor's policies vis-à-vis Haiti were actually more in the nation's best interests than the morally superior position he espoused as a candidate.

Repealing the repatriation policy still presented Haiti as a significant dilemma for President Clinton. In the period prior to his decision to conduct the September 1994 military intervention, the preferred means by which he determined to achieve his desired end of restoring democracy to Haiti were the use of an economic embargo and continuing multilateral negotiations. On the surface, the strategy seemed to fit nicely with the stated ends and means. The combination of economic and diplomatic pressures seemed like a sound recipe for success.[49] In retrospect, though, the strategy was flawed because the ends themselves were flawed.

Achieving democracy in Haiti required a dual effort from both the United States and Haiti. The United States could assist Haiti in the restoration of democracy by forcing the surrender of the military junta that monopolized Haitian power at the time; however, once a democratically elected government assumed power in Haiti, there was no guarantee that the elected government would act in a democratic manner. Moreover, the initial means to influence that end in the form of economic sanctions seemed to do more harm than good toward the average Haitian. In hindsight, the strategy of economic sanctions may have contributed to the achievement of the short-term end of restoring democracy in Haiti, but that same strategy also served as a tremendous impediment to the other stated end of producing stable conditions that fostered domestic development. By not fully grasping the cause and effects of economic sanctions, critics claim that the Clinton administration nearly destroyed Haiti in its attempt to save it.[50] In other words, the means employed were designed for the achievement of a short-term objective rather than the lasting ends as originally identified. Having the military junta relinquish their power in favor of a democratically elected government did promote democracy in the short-term, but it did not necessarily contribute to the long-term sustainment of democracy in Haiti—the real desired end of the United States regarding that country.

The 1994 U.S. intervention into Haiti encompassed several aspects of an ends-means mismatch. As previously stated, the principal stated end was the promotion of democracy in Haiti. The means to accomplish that end initially consisted principally of the implementation of economic sanctions. Often selected as a safe "middle ground" option, sanctions present the appearance of taking action without actually compelling tangible engagement. When applied to dictatorships, though, sanctions have proven repeatedly to do more harm to the populace than to the targeted regimes. In the case of Haiti, sanctions tended to merely exacerbate the hardship of the average Haitian and posed minimal inconveniences to the ruling elite. Tightening existing sanctions would have merely made the populace more miserable. However, while easing existing sanctions may have alleviated some of the citizens' suffering, that action would have also served the unintended purpose of perpetuating the dictatorship, thereby impeding the attainment of a central desired end and signaling the reversal of a foreign policy platform.[51]

As the ineffectiveness of the economic sanctions became more apparent, President Clinton decided that military action was necessary in order to achieve his administration's stated ends. Accordingly, he proposed the introduction of a 20,000-man interventional force.[52] The adjusted means to attain the desired ends required an intervention force, but the U.S. political climate indicated an aversion to the insertion of a substantial American force for a sustained period into Haiti. Therefore, on September 15, 1994, President Clinton addressed the nation in an attempt to shore up support for his proposed intervention into Haiti. His rationale for the action was that "The United States must protect its interests, to stop the brutal atrocities that threaten tens of thousands of Haitians; to secure our borders and to preserve stability and promote democracy in our hemisphere; and to uphold the reliability of the commitments we make and the commitments others make to us."[53] Other rationales for the intervention weighed on the President's mind as well and provided the final impetus required in the decision to commit military forces as the means to achieve the stated ends.

Among those additional rationales, the inability to solve the Haiti crisis presented a credibility challenge for the United States, and given the Clinton administration's multiple policy reverses to that point—i.e., the Haitian refugee policy, Bosnia, Somalia, etc.—the President was particularly sensitive to the fact that determined action was required regarding Haiti. Additionally, while a belief in altruism suggests that the U.S. decision to intervene in Haiti was made out of purely humanitarian concerns, reality indicates that the intervention was conducted due to more cynical reasons. Domestic political expediency rather than concern for humanitarianism or national interests appears to have guided the Clinton administration's policy regarding Haiti. Focused on an ambitious domestic agenda, the President saw Haiti as an inconvenient impediment that diverted attention away from his domestic platform. Accordingly, the quicker he could get Haiti resolved, the quicker he could resume his actual priorities.[54]

The end result was an intervention that achieved only temporary successes. As of this writing, Haiti's economy has not recovered, so in essence, the initial victory in Haiti celebrated by the Clinton administration appears to have been short-sighted. Once the military junta was removed from power, the will to continue with the necessary commitment of resources, i.e., the requisite means, to achieve the desired ends of democracy promotion and stability within Haiti seems to have departed with General Cedras. The Haitian leadership has proven unable to build upon the opportunity that the United States presented them in 1994, and the United States has proven uninterested in providing them with the necessary tools to help build their nation.[55]

Although the concept of nation-building has lost much of its luster recently, it remains a legitimate and fundamental component of the overall means by which the United States can achieve a critical stated end regarding Haiti☐ the creation of the conditions for stability necessary to foster an acceptable standard of living among the populace and thus reduce the burden on overall U.S. immigration.[56] Nation-building represents a long-term action designed to engender a long-term result. However, while the stated ends are long-term in focus, and the acknowledged means to achieve those ends are also long-term in focus, U.S. policy regarding Haiti has habitually indicated a focus on short-term objectives. In other words, while the ends and means often appear to match but in actuality do not, the strategy that binds them together is just as often inappropriate. Because the United States has refused to provide the necessary means to accomplish the ends regarding Haiti as stated in 1994, Haiti has continued to founder, teetering on the brink of collapse. The ends identified for Operation UPHOLD DEMOCRACY were indeed noble, but they demanded a long-term commitment that the U.S. leadership was not willing to endure. Consequently, the ends-means mismatch has resulted in at best a strategic purgatory regarding Haiti, with many believing that a repeat of the situation of the mid-1990s is inevitable.

Results were undeniably achieved in Haiti. U.S.-led reconstruction actions yielded positive results, and President Aristide was restored to power in an indication that democracy was restored to that island nation. However, the restoration of democracy required a lengthy commitment that the Clinton administration did not appear willing to embrace. Accordingly, while some short-term objectives were achieved, long-term ends were neglected when U.S. forces were prematurely withdrawn. The lack of success within the long-term domain can be attributed to the ends-means mismatch applied by the U.S. political leadership. An enduring democracy is indeed a noble end; however, if desired in a nation as fraught with developmental issues as Haiti is, that noble end must be accompanied by means reflective of that nobility.[57] The cessation of human rights abuses, the reconstruction of critical infrastructure, and the restoration of democratic principles could not endure because the means to perpetuate them were not sustained.

The lack of a coherent overarching strategy and the unwillingness to commit the requisite means to sustain the ambitious ends meant that success was fleeting in Haiti. If history is any guide, the failure to achieve lasting effects in Haiti will necessitate another U.S. intervention in the not too distant future.

Operation IRAQI FREEDOM and the Ends-Means Disconnect.

> A policy is pursued up to a certain point; it becomes evident at last that it can be carried no further. New facts arise which clearly render it obsolete; new difficulties which make it impracticable. A new and possibly opposite solution presents itself with overwhelming force. To abandon the old policy is often necessarily to adopt the new.

> Winston Churchill[58]

As of this writing, the U.S. venture in Iraq known as Operation IRAQI FREEDOM (OIF) continues in earnest. The war itself has proven to be a tremendously polarizing event both domestically and internationally, and there certainly is no lack of opinion regarding the necessity and utility of U.S. actions in Iraq. Two interrelated issues in particular seem to have bred the most vociferous contention — the perceived worth Iraq represents in terms of U.S. national interests and the debate regarding the existence of an ends-means mismatch in that conflict — and those are the issues on which this section focuses.

In the days prior to the commencement of hostilities, the debate over Iraq's relevance to the national interest predictably secured more attention than the disputes addressing ends and means. However, once the fight began, the latter issue gained substantial precedence within the national consciousness. Such a situation is understandable; the United States is involved in Iraq, and that reality is unlikely to change in the near future. Discussions regarding the proper place Iraq possesses within the pantheon of U.S. national interests, however, remain relevant because they are central to solving the second of those interrelated issues.

Even before combat actions were initiated, assertions abounded that inadequate means were applied to achieve the ends of OIF that have been and continue to be cited by President George W. Bush. As recently as January 10, 2007, the President admitted that an ends-means mismatch existed in Iraq when he stated that "there were not enough American troops" to achieve the tactical and operational successes necessary for the accomplishment of the strategic ends.[59] That statement is significant, and, strangely, one that received scant attention from the war's opponents who had been decrying what they viewed to be an insufficient commitment of forces to the conflict from the beginning.

In November of 2005, the White House produced a document entitled, *National Strategy for Victory in Iraq (NSVI)*. While many will argue that the *NSVI* was long overdue and much more appropriately conveyed prior to the commencement of hostilities, its publication is nonetheless significant. First, it declared in no uncertain terms that, "Victory in Iraq is a vital U.S. Interest."[60] Such a pronouncement carries substantial weight, for it implies that the use of American military force is determined necessary to achieve the desired ends inherent within that interest. Additionally, the administration's official ends were identified as the creation of an Iraq that is "peaceful, united, stable, and secure, well integrated into the international community, and a full partner in the global war on terrorism."[61] Further, the *NSVI* contained a section that articulated the specific U.S. strategy for achieving the desired ends. The strategy espoused the U.S. role in helping the Iraqi people, ". . . build a new Iraq with a constitutional, representative government that respects civil rights and has security forces sufficient to maintain domestic order and keep Iraq from becoming a safe haven for terrorists."[62] The strategy identified the requirement to pursue a comprehensive approach that synergizes the actions and capabilities of the governments of the United States, Iraq, and the coalition forces while also encouraging participation of the regional states, UN, and regional organizations in the process. Recognizing the requirement to synchronize the political, security, and economic aspects of national power, the *NSVI* devoted several pages to addressing the independent and integrated roles of each of those elements.

As seemingly detailed as the *NSVI* was, it was also incomplete. The six desirable characteristics of effective national strategies identified by the GAO mentioned earlier and referenced in Figure 2 were inadequately addressed.[63] Additionally, while strategy and ends were identified, the means to achieve those ends were never fully explained. Drafters of the *NSVI* might contend that such detail exceeded the scope of the document□s central purpose□ an articulation and summation of the administration□s overarching goals in Iraq. However, in order to be truly considered a coherent national strategy, the *NSVI* should have included at least a cursory examination of the means identified as necessary for the accomplishment of the stated ends. That way, effective analysis of the interrelationship among the ends, means, and overall strategy could occur, shortcomings could be rapidly identified, and suitable adjustments could be enacted. Most importantly, such analysis would contribute significantly toward ensuring balance among those three central elements of policy.

For example, within the security track articulated in the *NSVI*, specific referencing of the counterinsurgency tactic to "clear, hold, and build" was made. That particular tactic is relatively manpower intensive.[64] Therefore, one would infer that the inclusion of that tactic in the *NSVI* would have been followed by the allocation of adequate numbers of properly trained forces to achieve that stated end. For a strategy to be viable, the ends must be realistic and the requisite means to achieve those ends must be allocated. The President's contention in his January 2007 speech implies that there never was a match between ends and means regarding a key component of the overall end that addressed a stable Iraq. Addressing that discrepancy, he declared that, "this time we'll have the force levels we need to hold the areas that have been cleared."[65]

A recurring theme in the buildup to and within the text of the President's January 10, 2007, address is that the United States was embarking on a "new" strategy with regard to Iraq. However, such a proclamation may not be entirely accurate. The President's speech does not really signal a shift in strategy per se, primarily because the ends that the President identified in that address have not appreciably changed. In fact, the stated ends not only remain unchanged since they were presented in the *NSVI* some 14 months previously, they represent essentially the identical ends identified almost 4 years previously during the commencement of stabilization and reconstruction actions by coalition forces in 2003.[66] All of the changes identified in the President's address simply represent additional means to attain end states that have been previously identified. The additional means are represented by increased numbers of U.S. forces that will help the Iraqis pacify Baghdad, and the deployment of 18 Iraqi Army and National Police brigades in support of the overall Baghdad pacification effort. An increase in the number of embedded American advisers added resources to assist with reconstruction actions, including the doubling of Provincial Reconstruction Teams and accelerating the training of Iraqi Security forces, were also additional measures cited in the speech.[67] Ultimately, though, the declared ends from the beginning of OIF remain unchanged almost 4 years later. Moreover, the potential for a continuing ends-means mismatch remains within the security framework because success in that realm, particularly in Baghdad, assumes a level of proficiency among the Iraqi Security Forces that as yet remains unproven. The point here is that the requirement to allocate adequate means in support of a stated end is not necessarily a product of specific force numbers; competency of those forces is a significant factor in the overall analysis equation as well.

Further, as previously stated, policymakers must continually remain sensitive to changes within the operational and strategic environments that might necessitate reconsideration of stated ends. Vigilance is required to ensure that the conditions on the ground contribute to the continued legitimacy of the stated ends and that the attendant means and strategy remain in balance with those ends and with each other. In the specific case of Iraq, an argument can be made that the requisite analysis along those lines has not occurred, that the situation in Iraq is undeniably and radically different than it was in 2003, and that such a pronounced alteration to the operational and strategic environment necessitates a reevaluation of America⬚s stated ends along with an accompanying shift in overall strategy. What is beyond doubt, though, is that the environmental changes over the past 3 1/2 years in Iraq have undoubtedly nullified several of the key assumptions made at the beginning of stabilization and reconstruction actions.

The initial reconstruction plans provide ample evidence of the impact of flawed assumptions. A key assumption of the early reconstruction plan was that that Iraqi critical infrastructure, such as oil production capacity, electricity generation, and water treatment capabilities, would be rapidly restored to pre-war levels. However, the unstable security environment has not allowed any enduring, substantive repairs to be effected. Further compounding the difficulties of reconstruction, the anticipated dividends reaped from the Iraqi economy have never materialized as that nation has yet to realize significant export yields.[68] Additionally, the permissive environment on which reconstruction actions depend has yet to fully materialize. The lack of a secure overall environment created second and third order effects that have stymied and stultified many infrastructure repair projects and sharply limited the growth and development of provincial and national governmental capacity. Those situations have in turn hampered the central government's ability to harness legitimacy and acceptance among the Iraqi constituents and have served to embolden the various insurgent and sectarian groups that persist in asserting their respective positions while simultaneously undermining that of the Iraqi central government. The vicious cycle continues as the lack of security prevents further restoration actions, fostering further disillusionment among the populace and exacerbating the legitimacy problems for the central government. The question before policymakers is whether or not the significant changes in the strategic and operational environment mandate adjustments to the desired ends. As of this writing, the answer has been an unequivocal adherence to those ends with an accompanying recent adjustment to the means viewed as the best solution to the overall strategic dilemma. Time will tell if that methodology is effective.

Conclusion.

> To the Judge of Right and Wrong with Whom fulfillment lies our purpose and our power belong, our faith and Sacrifice
>
> Rudyard Kipling
> *The Choice*[69]

A nation sends a significant signal to the rest of the international community when it decides to commit interventional forces. Outside of asserting a requirement to defend the homeland, such an action expresses an undeniable intent that a nation is willing to sacrifice blood and treasure for the attainment of specified ends. Accordingly, clear, succinct, and obtainable ends must be articulated by national leadership prior to the commitment of force to ensure that force is actually representative of appropriate and corresponding means to achieve those ends. Moreover, only a unified strategic design can ensure that the means are properly employed and that the ends remain focused□ especially when the environment changes in such a way as to engender a necessary adjustment to those ends that require a commensurate adjustment in dedicated means as well.

Sound strategic vision enables policymakers to determine the comparative value of a specific commitment as weighed against other national interests. While individual actions and the circumstances of their initiation alter from administration to administration, the principal ethos of a nation remains relatively constant and thus provides strategic leadership with a convenient guide from which to operate. Adhering to core principles enables policymakers to craft correspondingly cognizant strategies representative of the nation's values. While this is especially true of democracies, nations practicing that form of government face a strange paradox when it comes to defining national interests and strategic vision. On the one hand, they represent the most ideal governments to construct a sensible and even inspiring strategic vision, yet on the other hand, the unique characteristics inherent to their system deliberately create significant obstacles toward the development of that vision.

In other words, the fundamental nature of democracies presents a formidable challenge to the nurturing of strategic vision among its leadership. National leadership operates within the context of short-term election cycles, and strategic vision by definition requires a long-term approach. Those seeking reelection face a daunting task in convincing constituents to commit to a series of potentially enduring sacrifices in the name of a leader's strategic vision, particularly when the tangible benefits of those sacrifices may not be immediately realized. Accordingly, political leadership tends to seek "quick wins" to shore up support for the longer term victories. In taking such an approach, though, the short-term "wins" may actually prove counterproductive to the long-term victory. A credible argument can be made that the 1994 U.S. venture fits that description, since virtually all economic growth and development initiated during that intervention appears to have either halted or even regressed. One can make similar cases

20

when addressing the after effects of the previous decade's U.S. action in Somalia and, to a lesser extent, in the Balkans as well. Enduring commitment was required to achieve the respective stated ends in those places, but when that level of commitment was deemed to be politically unpalatable, the ends were adjusted to accommodate a more acceptable and reduced commitment (i.e., means), earning "wins" that ultimately failed to adequately address the base issues that caused the situations in the first place. Long-term strategic vision regarding Haiti, the Balkans, and Somalia was sacrificed for the sake of domestic politics, and the situation in Iraq teeters on the edge of a similar fate as of this writing. Such a situation, however, certainly is not unique to those regions. Rather, that is simply reflective of the reality inherent in operating within a democracy. Thus, the real challenge to democracies is determining a method by which long-term strategic vision supported by a genuine commitment of requisite resources required to achieve that vision is not only encouraged but routine.

ENDNOTES

1. Carl von Clausewitz, *On War*, Michael Howard and Peter Paret, eds. and trans., Princeton: Princeton University Press, 1976, 1984, p. 579.

2. Niccolo Machiavelli, *The Art of War*, ed., trans., and with commentary by Christopher Lynch, Chicago: The University of Chicago Press, 2003, p. 158.

3. *National Strategy for Victory in Iraq*, Washington, DC: National Security Council, November, 2005, pp. 1-2.

4. B. H. Liddell Hart, *Strategy*, London: Faber & Faber Ltd., 1954, 1967, p. 322.

5. Dennis M. Drew and Donald M. Snow, *Making Twenty-First Century Strategy: An Introduction to Modern National Security Processes and Problems*, Maxwell Air Force Base, AL: Air University Press, 2006, p. 13.

6. Angelo Codevilla and Paul Seabury, *War: Ends and Means*, Washington, DC: Potomac Books, Inc., 2006, p. 91.

7. *Ibid.*

8. P. H. Liotta, "To Die For: National Interests and Strategic Uncertainties," in *Strategy and Force Planning*, Newport, RI: Naval War College Press, 2004, p. 114.

9. *Ibid.*

10. Drew and Snow, p. 33.

11. Michael I. Handel, *Masters of War: Classical Strategic Thought*, London: Frank Cass Publishers, 1992, 1996, 2001, pp. 311-312.

12. *Rebuilding Iraq: More Comprehensive National Strategy Needed to Help Achieve U.S. Goals*, Washington, DC: Government Accountability Office, 2006, p. 2.

13. Codevilla and Seabury, p. 251.

14. *Ibid.*, pp. 92-94.

15. *Ibid.*

16. *Ibid.*, pp. 84-85.

17. *Ibid.*, p. 85.

18. Marcus Aurelius, *Meditations*, A. S. L. Farquharson, trans. and ed., New York: Everyman's Library, 1992, p. 14.

19. *The United Nations and Somalia: 1992-1996-The United Nations Blue Books Series*, Vol. VIII, New York: Department of Public Information, United Nations, 1996, p. 42.

20. Codevilla and Seabury, pp. 84-89; Wikipedia: The Free Encyclopedia, "UNOSOM II," available at *en.wikipedia.org/wiki/UNOSOM_II*, accessed December 17, 2006.

21. Richard N. Haas, *Intervention: The Use of American Military Force in the Post-Cold War World*, Washington, DC: The Brookings Institution, 1999, p. 44.

22. *The United Nations and Somalia: 1992-1996*, pp. 42, 261-263.

23. Codevilla and Seabury, p. 289.

24. Specifically, Article 42 of Chapter VII of the UN Charter states that, "Should the Security Council consider that measures provided for in Article 41 would be inadequate or have proved to be inadequate, it may take such action by air, sea, or land forces as may be necessary to maintain or restore international peace and security. Such action may include demonstrations, blockade, and other operations by air, sea, or land forces of Members of the United Nations." This is the chapter of the UN Charter that specifically authorizes nations participating in UN operations to use force if deemed necessary.

25. Karin von Hippel, *Democracy by Force: U.S. Military Intervention in the Post-Cold War World*, Cambridge, United Kingdom: Cambridge University Press, 2000, pp. 60, 64.; *The United Nations and Somalia: 1992-1996*, pp. 42, 261-263.

26. John L. Hirsch and Robert B. Oakley, *Somalia and Operation Restore Hope: Reflections on Peacemaking and Peacekeeping*, Washington, DC: United States Institute for Peace Press, 1995, p. 111; *The United Nations and Somalia: 1992-1996*, pp. 42, 261-263.

27. Codevilla and Seabury, p. 290.

28. U.S.-UN Press Release 37-(93) dated March 26, 1993; Hirsch and Oakley, p. 111; von Hippel, p. 64.

29. Codevilla and Seabury, p. 290.

30. Haas, pp. 45, 269.

31. *Ibid.*, p. 45.

32. von Clausewitz, p. 607.

33. William J. Clinton, President of the United States of America, *Address to the Nation on Somalia*, October 7, 1993, available at *www.presidency.ucsb.edu/ws/index.php?pid=47180*, accessed January 3, 2007; Haas, pp. 46, 270.

34. Robert D. Kaplan, *Balkan Ghosts: A Journey Through History*, New York: Picador Press, 2005, p. xxi.

35. Haas, pp. 39, 41.

36. Ed Vulliamy, *Seasons in Hell: Understanding Bosnia's War*, New York: St. Martin's Press, 1994, pp. 122-123.

37. *Ibid.*, pp. 281-283.

38. Codevilla and Seabury, p. 294.

39. Haas, p. 41.

40. Codevilla and Seabury, p. 292.

41. John Lewis Gaddis, "And Now This: Lessons from the Old Era for the New One," Strobe Talbott and Nayan Chanda, eds., *The Age of Terror: America and the World After September 11*, New York: Basic Books, 2001, pp. 14-15.

42. *Ibid.*, p. 15.

43. *Ibid.*, p. 17.

44. James Monroe, *Seventh Annual Presidential Address to Congress*, Wikipedia: The Free Encyclopedia, "Monroe Doctrine," available at *en.wikipedia.org/wiki/Monroe_Doctrine*, accessed January 11, 2007.

45. Ernest H. Preeg, "What Are the Real U.S. Interests in Haiti?" *Haitian Frustrations: Dilemmas for U.S. Policy*, Washington, DC: Center for Strategic and International Studies, 1995, p. 7.

46. Codevilla and Seabury, p. 121.

47. Robert C. DiPrizio, *Armed Humanitarians: U.S. Interventions from Northern Iraq to Kosovo*, Baltimore: Johns Hopkins University Press, 2002, p. 94.

48. *Ibid.*

49. Elliot Abrams, "Haiti: Playing out the Options," *Haitian Frustrations: Dilemmas for U.S. Policy*, Washington, DC: Center for Strategic and International Studies, 1995, p. 71.

50. *Ibid.*

51. Codevilla and Seabury, p. 121.

52. Thomas Carothers, "Lessons for Policymakers," *Haitian Frustrations: Dilemmas for U.S. Policy*, Washington, DC: Center for Strategic and International Studies, 1995, pp. 117, 120.

53. DiPrizio, pp. 97-98.

54. *Ibid.*, pp. 101-102.

55. Haas, p. 159.

56. Preeg, p. 11.

57. James Dobbins, John G. McGinn, Keith Crane, Seth G. Jones, Rollie Lal, Andrew Rathmell, Rachel Swanger, and Anga Timilsina, *America's Role in Nation-Building: From Germany to Iraq*, Santa Monica: RAND Corporation Publishing, 2003, pp. 83-84.

58. Winston Churchill, "Policies Old and New," *Winston Churchill: His Wit and Wisdom*, London: Hyperion Books, undated copyright, p. 61.

59. George W. Bush, President of the United States of America, *President's Address to the Nation*, January 10, 2007, available at *www.whitehouse.gov/news/releases/2007/01/20070110-7.html*, accessed January 11, 2007.

60. *National Strategy for Victory in Iraq*, p. 4.

61. *Ibid.*, pp. 1, 3.

62. *Ibid.*, pp. 7-8.

63. *Rebuilding Iraq*, p. 3. The GAO Report acknowledges that three of the six characteristics were generally addressed, but the other three were only partially addressed. The tables that follow on pages 25 and 26, and sourced from the actual report, elaborate. Of note, the column labeled, "NSVI+7 documents" refers to the seven additional documents, classified and unclassified, that relate to the NSVI. Specifically, those seven documents are (1) the *National Security Presidential Directive 36*, May 2004, (2) *Multinational Forces-Iraq, MNF-I) Campaign Plan*, August 2004, (3) the *MNF-I/U.S. Embassy Baghdad Joint Mission Statement on Iraq*, December 2005, (4) *Multinational Corps-Iraq Operation Order 05-03*, December 2005, (5) the *National Strategy for Supporting Iraq*, updated January 2006, (6) the quarterly *State Section 2207* reports to Congress through April 2006, and (7) the April 2006 *Joint Campaign Plan* issued by the Chief of Mission and the Commander of the MNF-I.

64. Headquarters, Department of the Army, and Headquarters, Marine Corps Combat Development Command, Department of the Navy, Field Manual No. 3-24 and Marine Corps Warfighting Publication No. 3-33.5, *Counterinsurgency*, Washington, DC: U.S. Government Printing Office, 2006, pp. 5-18, 5-23.

65. Bush.

66. *Rebuilding Iraq*, p. 3.

67. Bush.

68. *Rebuilding Iraq*, p. 3.

69. Rudyard Kipling, "The Quest," *Rudyard Kipling's Verse: Definitive Edition*, Garden City: Doubleday and Company, Inc., 1940, p. 520.

Extent the U.S. Strategy for Iraq Addresses GAO's Desirable Characteristics of an Effective National Strategy	NSVI	NSVI + 7 documents
1. Clear purpose, scope, methodology		
Purpose		
1a. Identifies the impetus that led to the strategy being written, such as a statutory requirement, mandate, or key event.	○	●
1b. Discusses the strategy's purpose.	●	●
Scope		
1c. Defines or discusses key terms, major functions, mission areas, or activities the strategy covers.	●	●
Methodology		
1d. Discusses the process that produced the strategy, e.g., what organizations or offices drafted the document, whether it was the result of a working group, or which parties were consulted in its development.	○	◐
1e. Discusses assumptions or the principles and theories that guided the strategy's development.	●	●
2. Detailed discussion of problems, risks, and threats		
Problem definition		
2a. Includes a detailed discussion or definition of the problems the strategy intends to address.	◐	●
2b. Includes a detailed discussion of the causes of the problems.	◐	◐
2c. Includes a detailed discussion of the operating environment.	●	●
Risk assessment		
2d. Addresses a detailed discussion of the threats at which the strategy is directed.	●	●
2e. Discusses the quality of data available, e.g., constraints, deficiencies, and "unknowns."	○	◐
3. Desired goals, objectives, activities, and performance measures		
Goals and subordinate objectives		
3a. Addresses the overall results desired, i.e., an "end-state."	●	●
3b. Identifies strategic goals and subordinate objectives.	●	●
Activities		
3c. Identifies specific activities to achieve results.	●	●
Performance measures		
3d. Addresses priorities, milestones, and outcome-related performance measures.	◐	◐
3e. Identifies process to monitor and report on progress.	●	●
3f. Identifies limitations on progress indicators.	○	○

● Addresses
◐ Partially addresses
○ Does not address

Source: GAO analysis of NSC, State, and DOD data.

	HSPI	NSVI + 7 documents
Extent the U.S. Strategy for Iraq Addresses GAO's Desirable Characteristics of an Effective National Strategy		
4. Description of future costs and resources needed		
Resources and investments		
4a. Identifies what the strategy will cost.	○	◐
4b. Identifies the sources, e.g., federal, international, and private, and types of resources or investments needed, e.g., budgetary, human capital, information technology, research and development, and contracts.	○	◐
Risk management		
4c. Addresses where resources or investments should be targeted to balance risks and costs.	○	◐
4d. Addresses resource allocation mechanisms.	○	◐
4e. Identifies risk management principles and how they help implementing parties prioritize and allocate resources.	○	○
5. Delineation of U.S. government roles and responsibilities		
Organizational roles and responsibilities		
5a. Addresses who will implement the strategy.	◐	●
5b. Addresses lead, support, and partner roles and responsibilities of specific federal agencies, departments, or offices, e.g., who is in charge during all phases of the strategy's implementation.	○	◐
Coordination		
5c. Addresses mechanisms and/or processes for parties to coordinate efforts within agencies and with other agencies.	◐	◐
5d. Identifies process for resolving conflicts.	○	○
6. Description of strategy's integration among and with other entities		
6a. Addresses how the strategy relates to the strategies of other institutions and organizations' and their goals, objectives, and activities (horizontal).	○	◐
6b. Addresses integration with relevant documents from other agencies and subordinate levels (vertical).	○	◐

● Addresses
◐ Partially addresses
○ Does not address

Sources: GAO analysis of NSC, State, and DOD data.